MW01173327

MAUVE

A Message From the Author

Much like the color mauve was discovered by accident, Maritza Holley is a poet that stumbled onto her poetic gift by accident. She discovered that she was gifted at poetry and rapping through class assignments. She began writing poetry often as a teenager while attending Savannah State University. Her first poetry book entitled 'Poetry as the Ultimate Cure' was never published due to her becoming a Christian. Once becoming a Christian Maritza decided that she no longer wished to share poems with vulgar language with others. Mauve is filled with poetry that the everyday person can relate to. With a goal of being relatable, inspiring, comforting, or even bringing insight, Mauve is the first project of many to come.

Acknowledgements

I would first like to say thank you to God! Thank you for turning my life around. Thank you for the gifts you have given me. May I steward them well. Thank you to anyone who has ever prayed for me. Thank you to anyone who has ever loved me. For with love and prayer alone one can accomplish much. Thank you to my supportive husband, Jerry who is always in my corner. Thank you for believing in me. Thank you to my mother who has helped us greatly along the way and for being a great role model. I would also like to say thank you to Apostle Graham and Prophetess Anita for everything that you have poured into us. I am forever grateful for your yes. Lastly, to my readers and supporters, thank you all. I hope this poetry collection adds to your life. May the blessings of God overtake you all.

Dedication

For African American girls everywhere including my four.
"Believe you can achieve."

To Kereneke Deterville Donelly

For seeing in me what I could not see. You supported my work way back when. I don't know where you are or if you even remember me, but you are the kind of person people need in their life! I'm so glad we crossed paths. Thank you for motivating me to stick with it. We can never underestimate the power of positive words and actions.

True Champion

I wonder if anyone has ever told you you're a champion

You see a champion keeps pushing no matter what is happening

When no one else is watching, they push and they press

When life gets hard, they rise to the challenge, eyes set on success

A champion commits and doesn't quit

When the road gets rocky, they get Balboa with the hits

Through trials and tribulations, they strive to prevail

Even in losses, they don't see it as a fail

They learn from it all

They get back up and fight when they stumble, trip, and fall

When I look at you, I see a champion

Always remember that no matter what is happening.

Price Far Above Rubies

Renee Brown, a true gem indeed.

But price far above rubies,

If you know what I mean.

Such a beautiful soul,

Loved and cared for so many.

Would give you her last, down to the penny.

Prayer warrior,

That describes her to a T.

She always desired to see those around her set free.

Leading others to Christ, in the midst of her own trials.

When searching for hope we knew the number to dial.

404 488 7292,

She might not know the answer, but she would pray for you.

Constantly speaking life, to the broken and defeated

Reeling um' in, she understood life's meaning

Loved ones all around will always miss her deeply

But we're glad she's gone on home,

No more sorrow, pain, or weeping.

A blessed woman, left us faith a great inheritance

Thank the Lord for our time together,

May we forever treasure it!

Renee Brown, a true gem indeed.

But price far above rubies,

If you know what I mean.

For Evangelist Renee Brown, an awesome woman of God, and powerful intercessor.

Regrets

If I could turn back the hands of time

I would have answered every call

Enjoyed every moment

Embraced every lesson

Took it all in

But I did not

Could not

Would not, understand

What I now wish I'd understood

Gospel Juke Box

I must be a gospel jukebox.

I know you may not hear it,

But there's a song playing in my spirit,

And I won't press stop.

I hear songs of worship,

I hear songs of praise,

I hear songs of hope,

Gets me through hard days.

I hear songs of encouragement,

I hear songs of freedom and deliverance,

And nothing seems to hinder it.

I hear old songs,

I hear new songs,

Forgot all about you songs.

Sometimes I like to sing along.

This morning it started when I woke up.

I hear a song of forgiveness,

I hear a song of appreciation,

I too am thankful for His mercy.

I have dreams

I'm no Nikki G

But I've got big aspirations

Inspiring people all over the nation

I'm no Maya Angelou

But I've got places to go

No one can stop me, neither friend nor foe

I'm no Madam CJ Walker

But I've got drive

To make something of myself while I am alive

I'm no Rosa Parks

But I'm here for a purpose

No matter what they say, I Know I am not worthless

I'm no Jackie Robinson

But I strive to do my best

There's things I want to achieve, I won't settle for less

I'm no Muhammad Ali

But I keep fighting

I cannot give up, I must keep on trying

I'm no Frederick Douglas

But I want you to know

I believe in myself, and I got big goals

I'm no Martin Luther King

But I've got big dreams

To make a difference

And do great things

A New Perspective

I'm okay with her being intelligent,

And you should be too.

I'm okay with her being anointed,

And you should be too.

I'm okay with her being established,

And you should be too.

I'm confident in who I am,

And you should be too.

I'm okay with her being well-read,

And you should be too.

I'm okay with her being educated,

And you should be too.

I'm okay with her being successful,

And you should be too.

I'm confident in who I am,

And you should be too.

I'm okay with her looking nice,

And you should be too.

I'm okay with her being a good singer,

And you should be too.

I'm okay with her being a good cook,

And you should be too.

I'm confident in who I am,

And you should be too.

I'm proud of the woman I've become

I may not be where I want to be,

but I'm proud of the woman I've become.

I may not be where I thought I would be,

but I'm proud of the woman I've become.

I may not be where others think I should be,

but I'm proud of the woman I've become.

I may not be where I will be,

but I'm proud of the woman I've become.

Keep on Writing

Through the difficulties you face

Just keep on writing

Through hard times

People have always kept on writing

Through adversities

They kept on writing

In turbulent times

They kept on writing

It is resilience

It is strength

It is worth it

So keep on writing

2 Pretty Apples

I bought some apples

And boy did they look delicious

They looked beautiful

Nice, shiny, and red

I was excited to eat them

Until I cut them open

Rotten spots?

How could I have missed this?

They did not taste good

They were going bad

But they looked so beautiful

Nice, shiny, and red

In life

Everything's

Not what it seems

Tread carefully on this journey we call life

Or you might be tricked by what looks right

It's what's on the inside that counts!

You should never judge a book by it's cover

But never take the time to discover

The treasure on the inside

Often hidden from the eye

Though the outside, it is nice to see

It's what on the inside that counts most to me!

Hold your head up

They may look down on me

But when I open up my mouth, then they see

Inner beauty and value

Richer than the producers of Calilou

My outer appearance has them confused

How could someone like her be used

But fancy clothes don't make God move

And he doesn't pick you based on your shoes

Man may ignore you based on what you got

But I'm so glad that God does not

He's not impressed by the car in the yard

Or the 6 figure job you're about to start

One thing I have learned is He can use you where you are

In His eyes you are a star

See you may live with your mother, so you feel like you're nothin'.

They're driving nice cars and you're using buses.

People, see people they may treat you like nothin'.

But always remember, in God's eyes you're somethin'!

Laughter in the distance

I hear laughter in the distance

Those women are having a blast

As I listen through the window

I feel sort of sad

Maybe a bit envious

Maybe even a bit mad

I can hear them from way across the way

I didn't know grey clouds were in the forecast today

It sounds like they're having the time of their lives

I wanna be laughing

With other mothers and wives

But what has my day consisted of?

Bath giving, breakfast making, caretaking.

No laughter with friends

I wonder will I experience friendship again

I know I will, but in this moment I doubt

Being a mother sure will make you feel you're missing out

And sometimes you will be

But know it's temporary.

Rebuttal's

"I don't got nobody."

You have God.

"Nobody's there for me."

God is there for you.

"Don't nobody care about me."

God cares about you.

"I can't count on nobody."

You can count on God.

"Nobody loves me."

God loves you…

Note to self

Some people don't care for you, but some people absolutely love you. So why would you waste precious time being concerned about who's not in your life instead of celebrating who is. As some say, "their loss". Who's not in your corner is not as important as who is. Rest in the fact that all you have is all you need and don't stress about the rest. If it comes cool but if not so be it.

Moving on

There's a few women I've really wanted to be friends with

Women of God mainly

One I may never meet

A famous poet

The others I won't name

I really wanted to connect

But one day I woke up and it no longer mattered as much

Didn't quite care as much anymore

No longer desired to connect

I was finally okay

Free

For now at least

I guess it would be nice

But for now I am at peace with what is

And what isn't

In My Hood (A poem about my experiences in majority African American Communities)

In my hood they wear bonnets, lashes, and long nails.

Some got degrees,

Some fresh outa jail.

You see a few fancy cars,

Not a lot though.

We rock braids and dreads,

Most don't wear the fro' no mo'.

We wear sneakers and hoodies.

When the ice cream truck comes through,

The kids run and ask for money.

Sometimes we see adults riding on a kid bike.

And the bus still be running through at midnight.

The bus stops be packed,

The wing spots do too.

Somebody bound to walk up,

Asking can they pray for you.

You can catch us at the library reading,

Or at the church interceding.

They gone tell you bout Jesus and feed ya.

Tell you stay outa trouble cause your kids really need ya.

The drive throughs take a long time,

They be yelling through the speaker.

They be talking kinda rude,

I don't think they glad to see ya.

We like to throw meat on the grill, wheneva.

We say things like "I'm out here getting that cheddar".

They be grilling and selling plates,

Whether hot or cold.

Where they wash their hands, nobody knows.

We put meat in our baked beans,

Our teachers had names like Mrs. Johnson and Mrs. Green.

We support each other even when we're down on our luck,

The Old heads sell fruit out the back of their truck.

Ain't nobody even trippin,

We got rappers, poets, and politicians.

We got teachers and preachers that don't get mentioned,

We got people that come up with creative inventions.

You can get your hair cut and your screen fixed,

If you look on the shelf you gone see old school picts.

We stock up on noodles.

You see a lot of pitbulls, not poodles.

We grew up watching Comic View, Martin, and Fresh Prince.

At church the older ladies had a purse full of mints.

Our daughters wear beads,

Our pastors kind of hood,

Church is kind of long but the choirs always good.

Our sons real athletic.

The soul food, authentic,

If you come to our reunions, you will not forget it.

The grandma's got gold teeth,

The OG's got 4 teeth,

Be careful who you try, or you might leave with no teeth.

We got Bible's in the car,

We accept you where you are,

But please don't bring the mac and cheese if it ain't up to par.

We believe in God but it don't always show,

You gone see a cross on the wall, or a picture of Jesus when you walk through the do'.

It's more than one meaning when we ask "are you good",

For the most part it's all love, in my neighborhood.

In my hood, A celebration of black culture. Shoutout to all the black neighborhoods.

Something to think about

In life I've made some bad choices. But haven't we all? We don't have to stay there. We've all made bad decisions but the difference between some people is that they learn from them instead of letting it define them. Sometimes it feels like all hope is lost but that's not always true. Just something to think about.

Unpleasant College Memories

I was drawing in class.

Not just any class,

A college class.

I drew the guy with his hand raised.

I drew the board and the picture of Nikki Giovanni.

I was uninterested.

I hated college.

Now I wish I could turn back the hands of time,

But I can't.

I wonder is there a rewind button,

But there ain't.

Such is life.

What day is it??

Hellos

Goodbyes

Drop Offs

Pick ups

Sign ins

Sign outs

Emails

Voicemails

Clothes Ironing

Dishwashing

Grocery store runs

Library visits

Commutes

Traffic

Doctor's visits

Dental visits

Cooking

Hair washing

Braiding

Gas stations stops

Homework

Arguments

Bath time

Story time

Repeat

What day is it??

RSVP

I missed it because I was tired

I missed it because I didn't have transportation

I missed it because I didn't have gas money

I missed it because I didn't have anything nice to wear

I missed it because my hair wasn't done

I missed it because I didn't have a babysitter

I did not miss it because I didn't miss you

I did not miss it because I didn't care

You were mad that I missed it

Took it personal when I missed it

Took it as dismissive

I should have told you I would miss it

But some things are hard to communicate

I missed out when I missed it

I was disappointed that I missed it

I missed a lot of things

Seems like I missed everything

But I grew when I missed it

I got stronger when I missed it

God was doing something in me when I missed it

Now I don't regret missing it

Fried Apples

My grandmother made the best fried apples

Butter, cinnamon, sugar

Apples from the tree in her backyard

Our job was to pick the apples

I can still smell um'

I still remember the taste

The restaurants don't come close to hers

I tried, mine don't either

How could this be?

Didn't she use the same ingredients as me?

What sugar did she use?

What butter?

I had all the ingredients, except one

Her

What I would do to taste them again

It's important to enjoy the moment

We had some good times didn't we?

Back then

Though I miss those days I have to move on.

It's fall

Fall is here.

It's time to mix up corn bread,

Onions,

Chicken stock,

Celery,

Chicken or turkey,

Salt,

Pepper,

And sage,

And make our favorite dish.

Dressing,

Some call it Southern Cornbread Dressing.

Let's get to cooking,

I can taste it now!

Kitchen Woes

I tried to make my grannies fried apples,

They didn't come out that well.

I tried to make homemade biscuits,

They didn't come out that well.

I tried to make gravy,

It didn't come out that well.

I'll get it one day!

I tried to get people to understand me,

It didn't turn out that well.

I tried to make friends,

It didn't turn out that well.

I tried to make ends meet,

It didn't turn out that well.

I'll get it one day!

An Aunts Kindness

Each Christmas she would send me a little check in the mail

So now the world I want to tell

I want to tell you a story about 10 dollars

That little check for 10 dollars must've traveled for hours

From Cleveland to Georgia

Crossing state borders

Now her act of kindness will travel with me

I will tell my children of my thoughtful Auntie

An aunt I barely knew

Chose to do something she didn't have to do

As an adult I let her know, I appreciated her deed

It meant the world to me indeed

It sure does feel good to be thought of

And it's a blessing when someone takes the time to show you love

For Aunt Helen

Memories

Sitting around with family,

Playing with cousins,

Laughing and joking around,

"Joning" "Janking" "Roasting"

(Whatever you wanna call it),

Meeting new relatives,

Eating cake and pie,

Playing outside, getting all dirty…

I don't wish to go back,

But I truly miss that.

To my unborn daughter

I'm gonna love you chile'…

Mommy can't wait to see you smile

I know we'll have lots of fun and laughs

Good food, love, and photographs

I look forward to the good times

Just can't wait to let you hear my rhymes

Hmm, I wonder how you'll be

I wonder will you be anything like me

Will you have a gentle side

But at the same time a roar

That could make a tiger hide

Will you be so darn funny

You could make a wall laugh

Or will you be a little scholar

Excelling in math

Either way I'm so excited

That I cannot even hide it

I'm gonna love you chile'…

Mommy can't wait to see you smile!

For Cade

On bringing families together

Big dinner,

Lots of food,

Pound cake,

Sodas,

Card games,

Music,

Fun & laughter,

That oughta bring um togetha'.

Now all you need is a big scoop of love,

A little bit of kindness,

And a whole lot of patience,

Now that'll really bring um togetha'

Feeling Alone

I've been feeling alone lately,

But I know I'm not alone.

No one to connect with,

No one to call me on the phone.

I wonder why I'm feeling this way,

Haven't felt this in a while.

Because I always remember God is with me,

and that's enough to make me smile.

Be careful what you say

It's always important,

To be careful what you say.

A friend yesterday,

Might not be a friend today.

Wondering what happened,

And if everything's okay?

Not knowing that it was our words,

That ran them right away.

Keep On Going

Disappointments don't feel good,

But keep on going.

Losses don't feel good,

But keep on going.

Failure doesn't feel good,

But keep on going.

You may bend but not break,

So, keep on going.

You got a lot to live for,

So, keep on going.

I hope

I hope you have a bright future

Though life won't always be easy

I hope things go good for you

Though some days will be rainy

I hope you feel complete

I hope you feel whole

I hope you never have to question your role

I hope you feel valued

I hope you feel loved

I hope you rely on the Man Up Above

I hope you succeed

I hope you win

I hope you can look back and smile in the end

Set Apart

I am a child of God and I am called to be set apart

Not walk in the dark

God wants me to live for Him out loud

Not follow the crowd

My friends may go one way, my family another

But I must follow Christ, not my brother.

People may think I'm strange for doing things God's way

But they wouldn't if they knew He was the potter and we are the clay

He created us to worship Him

And let our lights shine bright, not dark and dim

So, if they wonder why

I won't be shy

I will tell them why I want to be different

And I hope that they will listen

I am a child of God and I am called to be set apart

Not walk in the dark

God wants me to live for Him out loud

Not follow the crowd

The Prayer Warrior

I thank God for the prayer warrior.

Thank you to all the prayer warriors for...

Praying for the sick and the broken,

Praying for the hopeless,

Praying for the homeless,

Praying for our communities,

Praying for our futures,

Praying for the widows,

Praying for the orphans,

Praying for our country.

For this I say, Thank you.

Don't give up

In this life we have to fight.

And we don't have to pretend everything's alright.

Trials and tribulations may come and visit,

But it's not the end when God is with you in it.

So, when despair comes to visit,

Look it in it's face and put it in it's place.

When depression rings the bell,

Let it know it won't prevail.

When hopelessness knocks on the door,

Remind yourself of the things God has in store.

Life is filled with ups and downs,

Some seasons seem to have more frowns than smiles.

We've all made mistakes,

Some have hit rock bottom.

But God can help us through,

Don't forget about Him.

Lean on Him with everything you got.

He'll be there with you even when you feel He's not.

So please keep fighting the good fight of faith,

For just up ahead, something beautiful awaits.

About the Author

Maritza Holley is a Christian, wife, and mother of four young children. She was born and raised in Georgia where she currently resides. Her hobbies include thrifting and trying new recipes. She also enjoys reading, writing, good conversations, and listening to gospel music.

Made in the USA
Columbia, SC
25 August 2024

41121032R10030